CONCERT FAVORITES

Volume 2

Band Arrangements Correlated with Essential Elements 2000 Band Method Book 1

Page	Title	Composer/Arranger	Correlated with Essential Elements
2	Bandroom Boogie	Michael Sweeney	Book 1, page 11
3	Beethoven's Ninth	arr. Paul Lavender	Book 1, page 11
4	Gallant March	Michael Sweeney	Book 1, page 11
5	High Adventure	Paul Lavender	Book 1, page 11
6	Rock & Roll—Part II (The Hey Song)	arr. Paul Lavender	Book 1, page 11
7	Amazing Grace	arr. Paul Lavender	Book 1, page 24
8	Infinity (Concert March)	James Curnow	Book 1, page 24
9	Latin Fire	John Higgins	Book 1, page 24
10	Linus and Lucy	arr. Michael Sweeney	Book 1, page 24
11	Theme from "Star Trek® Generations"	arr. Michael Sweeney	Book 1, page 24
12	American Spirit March	John Higgins	Book 1, page 34
13	Gathering In The Glen	Michael Sweeney	Book 1, page 34
14	The Loco-Motion	arr. John Higgins	Book 1, page 34
15	Royal Fireworks Music	arr. Michael Sweeney	Book 1, page 34
16	Scarborough Fair	arr. John Moss	Book 1, page 34

ISBN 978-1-4234-0087-5

HAL•LEONARD®
CORPORATION

7777 W. BLUEMOUND RD. P.O. BOX 13819 MILWAUKEE, WI 53213

D1316940

00860175

BANDROOM BOOGIE

Tuba

Michael Sweeney

00860175

BEETHOVEN'S NINTH

3

Tuba

LUDWIG VAN BEETHOVEN
Arranged by PAUL LAVENDER

Lightly, with spirit

00860175

GALLANT MARCH

MICHAEL SWEENEY

TUBA

00860175

HIGH ADVENTURE

TUBA

PAUL LAVENDER

00860175

ROCK & ROLL - Part II
(The Hey Song)

Tuba

Words and Music by
MIKE LEANDER and GARY GLITTER
Arranged by PAUL LAVENDER

00860175

AMAZING GRACE

TUBA

Traditional American Melody
Arranged by PAUL LAVENDER

00860175

INFINITY
(Concert March)

JAMES CURNOW (ASCAP)

TUBA

00860175

LATIN FIRE

TUBA

JOHN HIGGINS

00860175

LINUS AND LUCY

By VINCE GUARALDI
Arranged by MICHAEL SWEENEY

Tuba

00860175

* New Note: G♭

THEME FROM "STAR TREK® GENERATIONS"

TUBA

Music by DENNIS McCARTHY
Arranged by MICHAEL SWEENEY

00860175

AMERICAN SPIRIT MARCH

JOHN HIGGINS

TUBA

00860175

GATHERING IN THE GLEN

TUBA

MICHAEL SWEENEY

THE LOCO-MOTION

**Words and Music by
GERRY GOFFIN and CAROLE KING**
Arranged by JOHN HIGGINS

Tuba

Rock Style

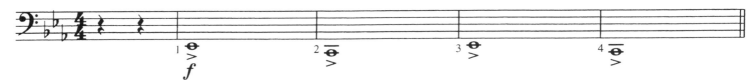

00860175

ROYAL FIREWORKS MUSIC

TUBA

GEORGE FREDERIC HANDEL
Arranged by MICHAEL SWEENEY

00860175

SCARBOROUGH FAIR

Tuba

Traditional English
Arranged by JOHN MOSS

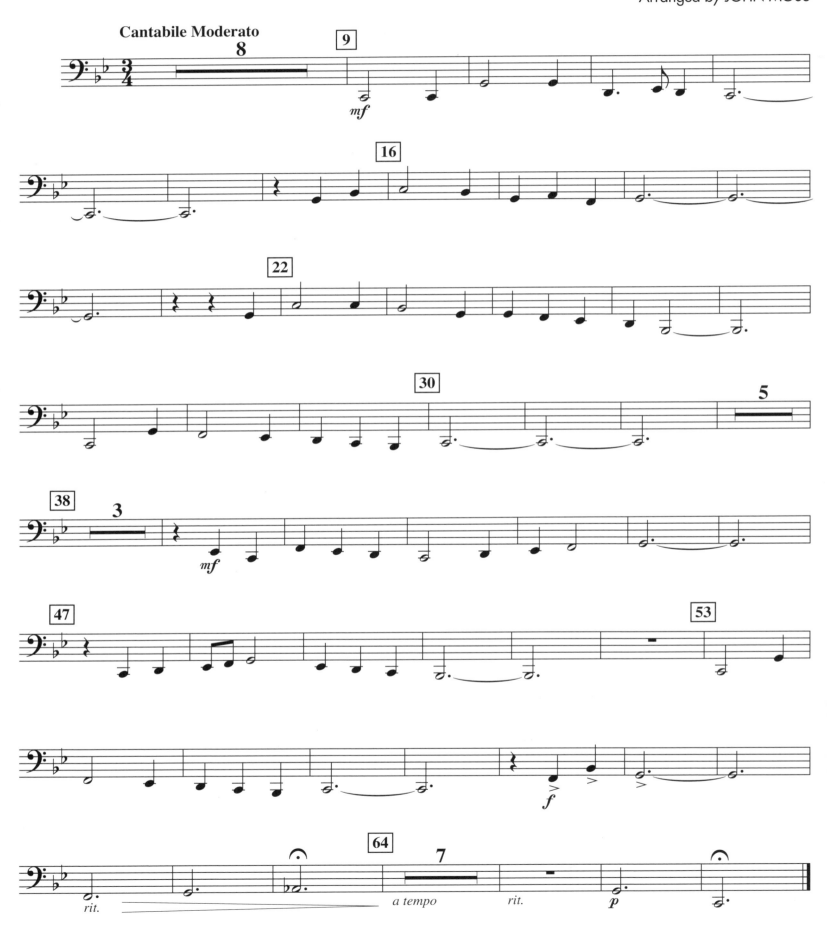